DUFFIELD BRANCH LIBRARY
2507 WEST GRAND BOULEVARD
DETROIT, MICHIGAN 48208
(313) 481-1712

APR - - 2023

DU

Tickle your Teeth

By Lauren Kelley
Illustrated by Emmy Mitchell

Copyright © 2017 by the author
and illustrator of this book -
Lauren Kelley and Emmy Mitchell.
All rights reserved. The book author
and illustrator retain joint copyright to
their contributions to this book.

My name is Baby Tooth!
Your mouth is my home.

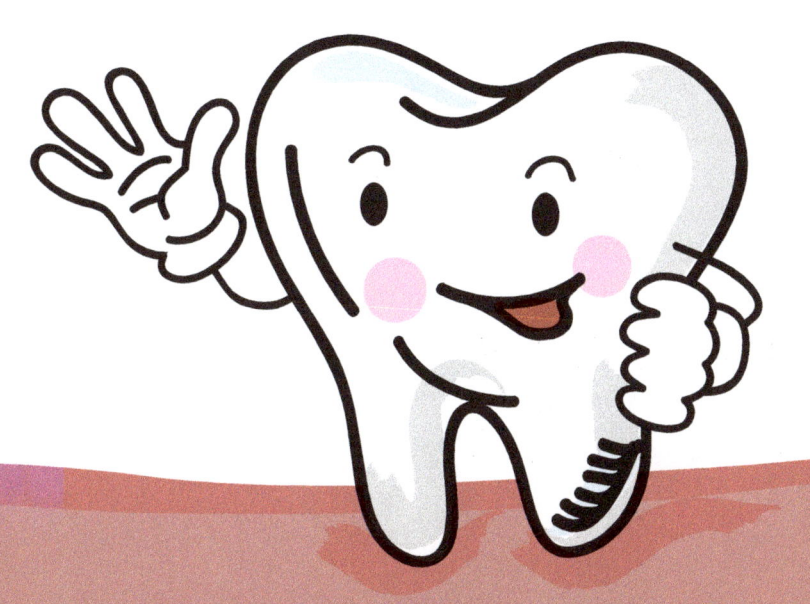

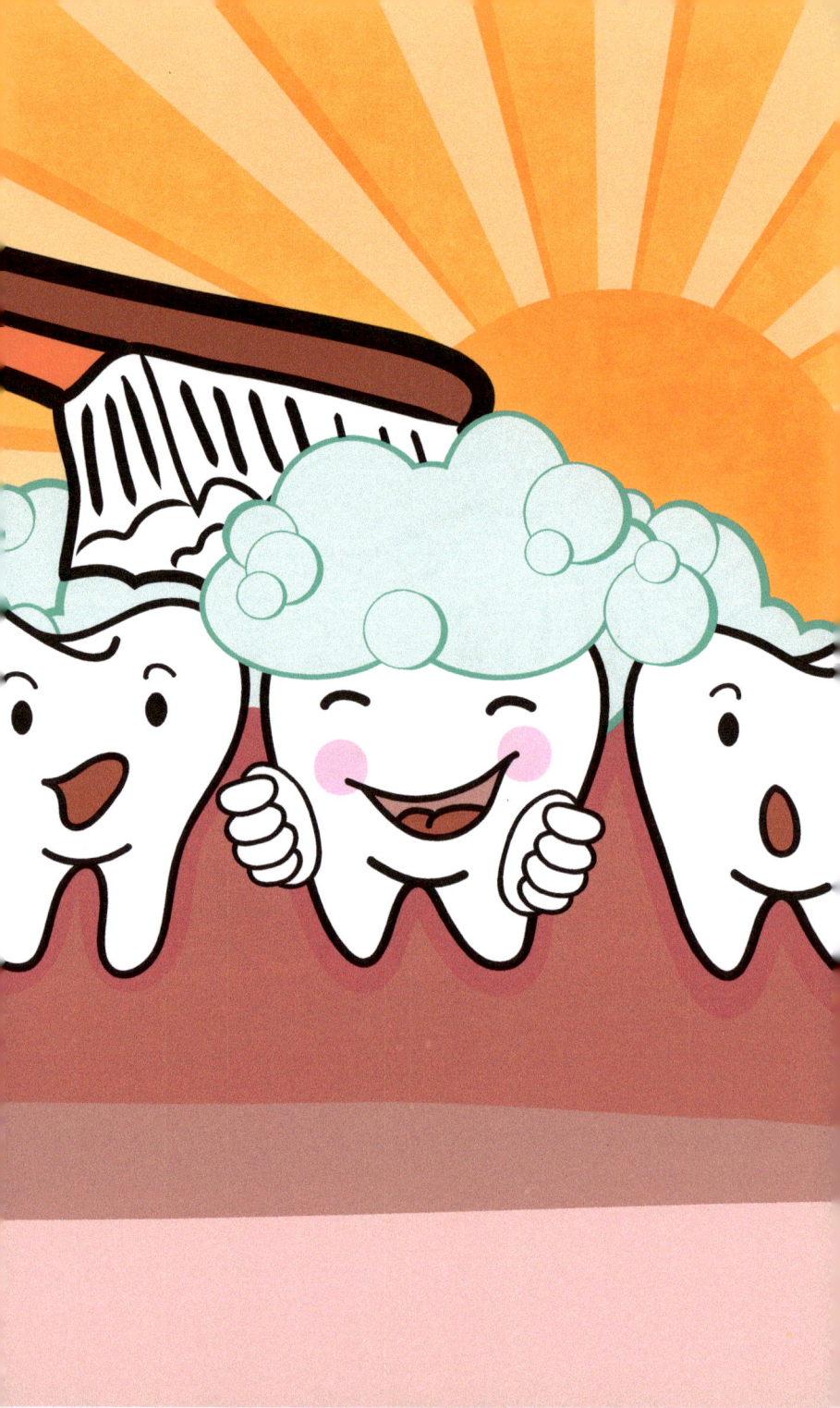

My favorite time is when you tickle me with your toothbrush!

In the morning...

And again at night!

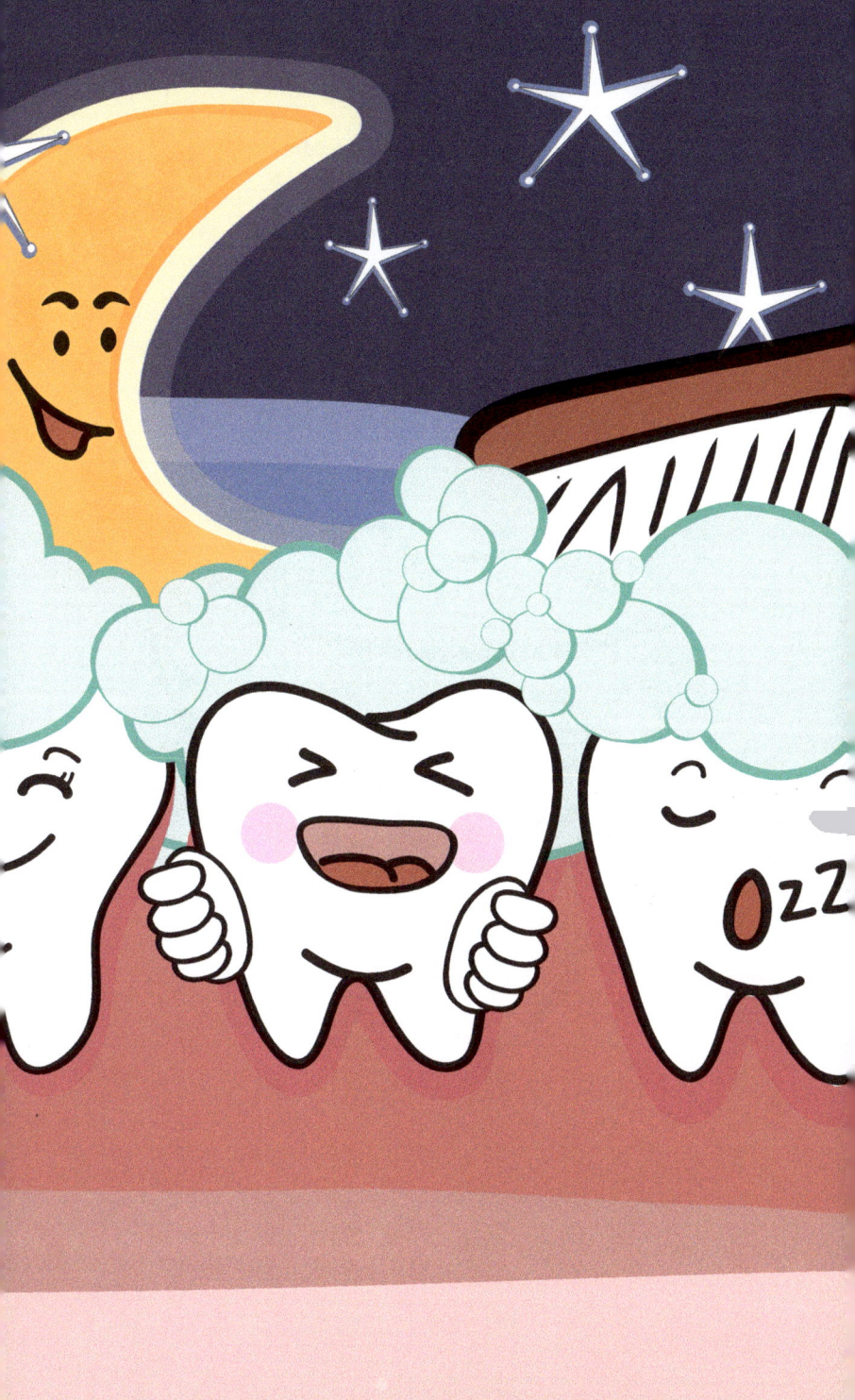

Haha, it tickles!

My job is to help you eat.

I chomp chomp chomp your food.

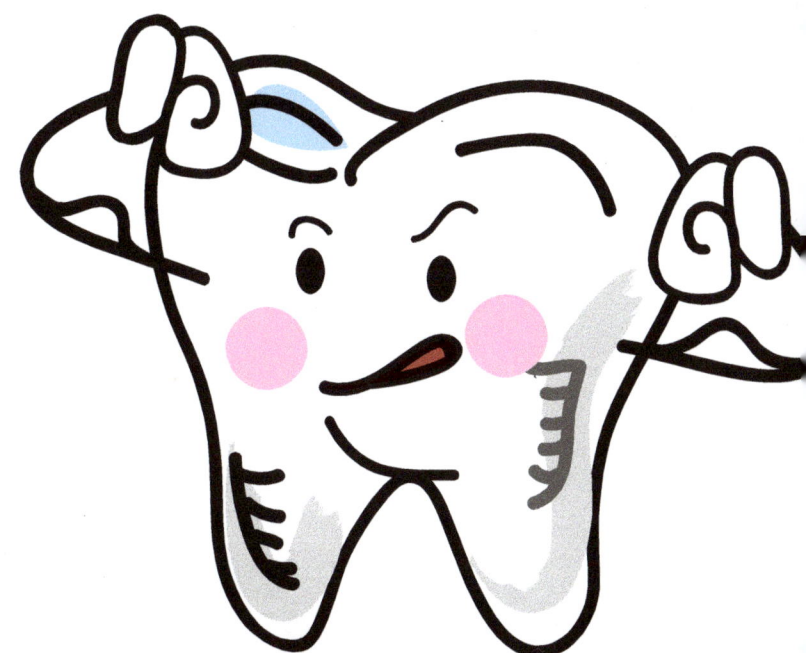

It's hard work. It makes me very dirty. Yuck!

If I stay dirty for too long,
I get sick with sugar bugs.

Ouch.

I want to be a healthy tooth! Will you please tickle me clean?

Round and round! Up and down! More bubbles!

Hehe!

I'm clean! Yay!

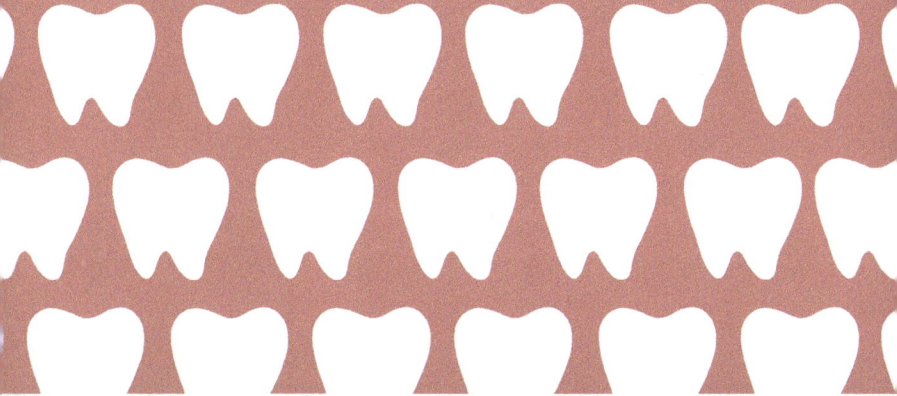

Don't miss out on teaching your child about good dental health! Check out the other books in this series: **Nutrition 101 With Baby Tooth**, **Baby Tooth Gets A Cavity**, and **Baby Tooth Meets The Tooth Fairy**. Available in select dental offices and online.

CPSIA information can be obtained
at www.ICGtesting.com
Printed in the USA
LVHW081804270323
742707LV00010B/381